This book belongs to

_____

_____

Thank you.
We hope you enjoyed our book.
As a small family company, your
feedback is very important to us.
Please let us know how you like our
book at:

calendulabooks@gmail.com

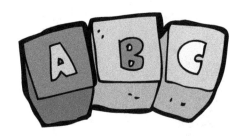

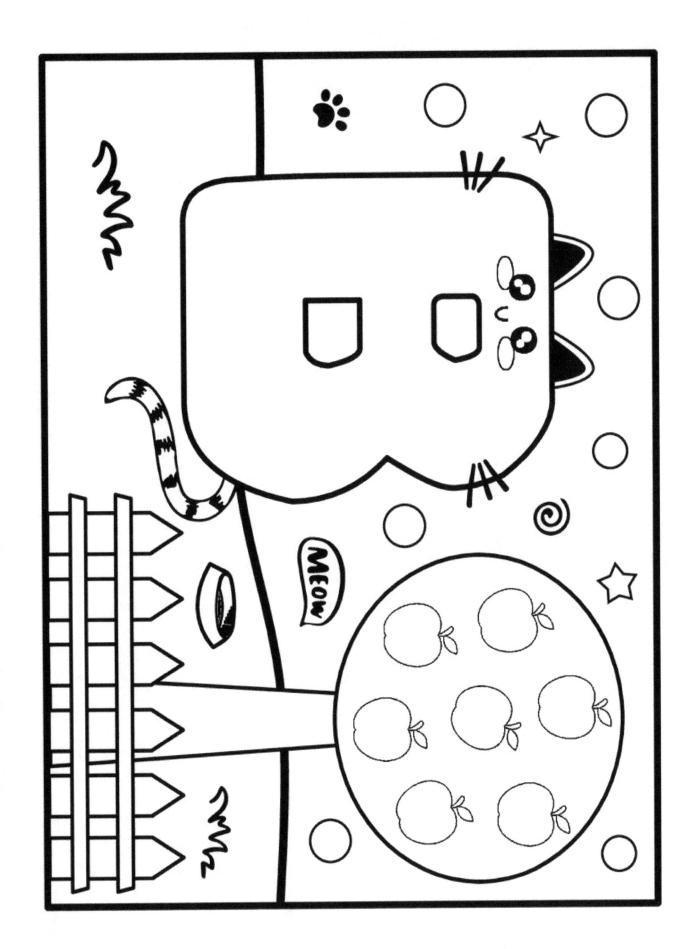

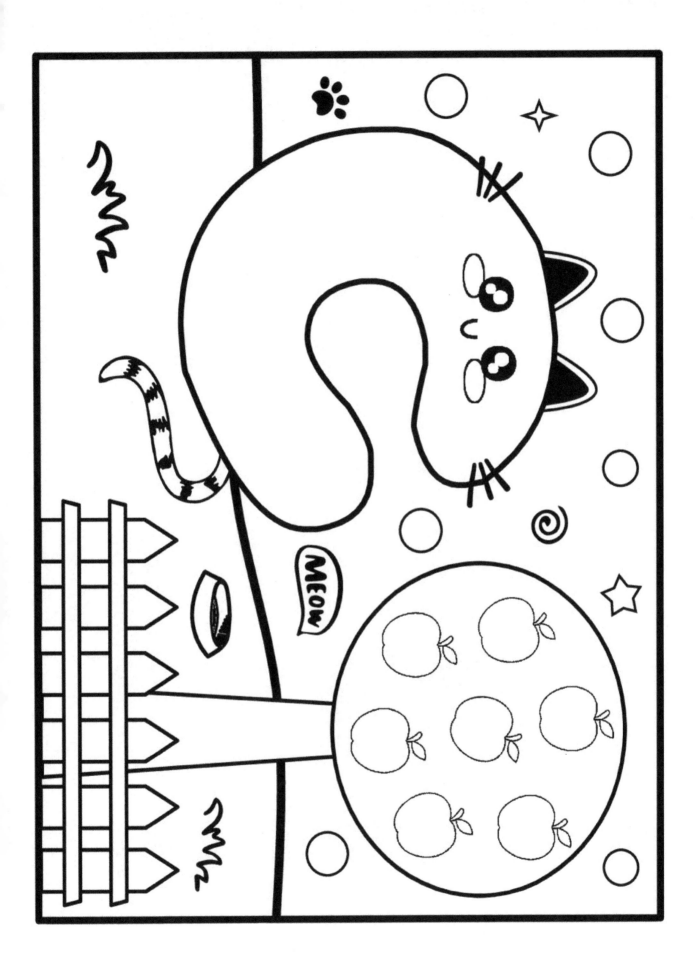

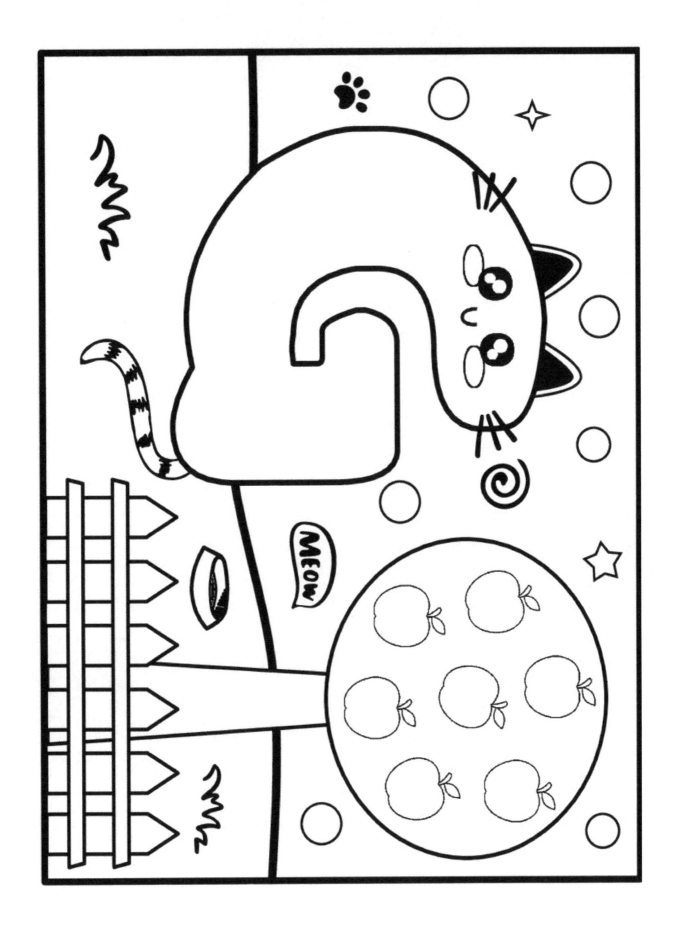

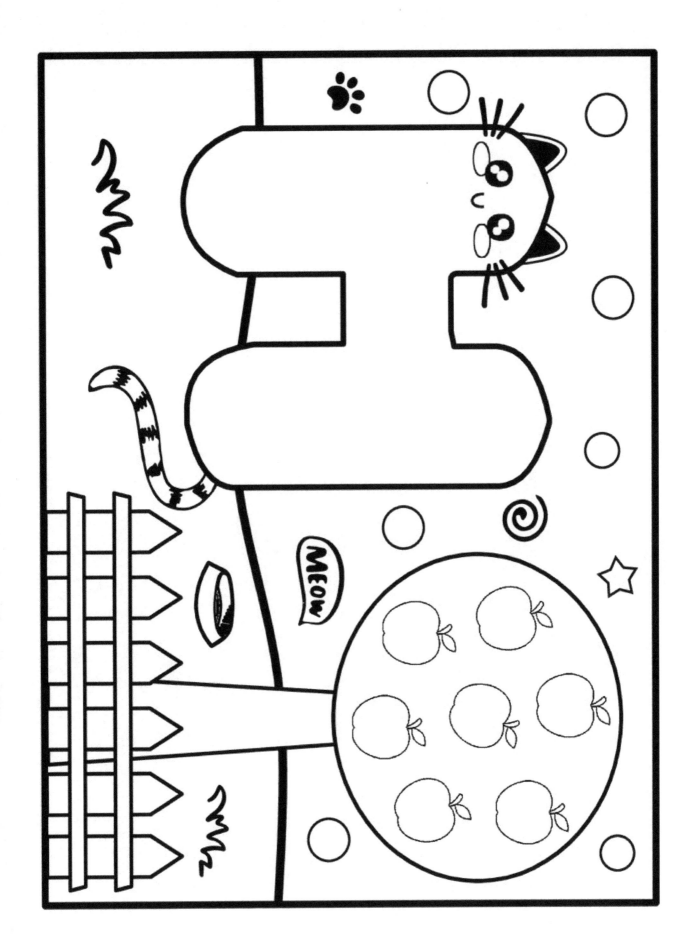

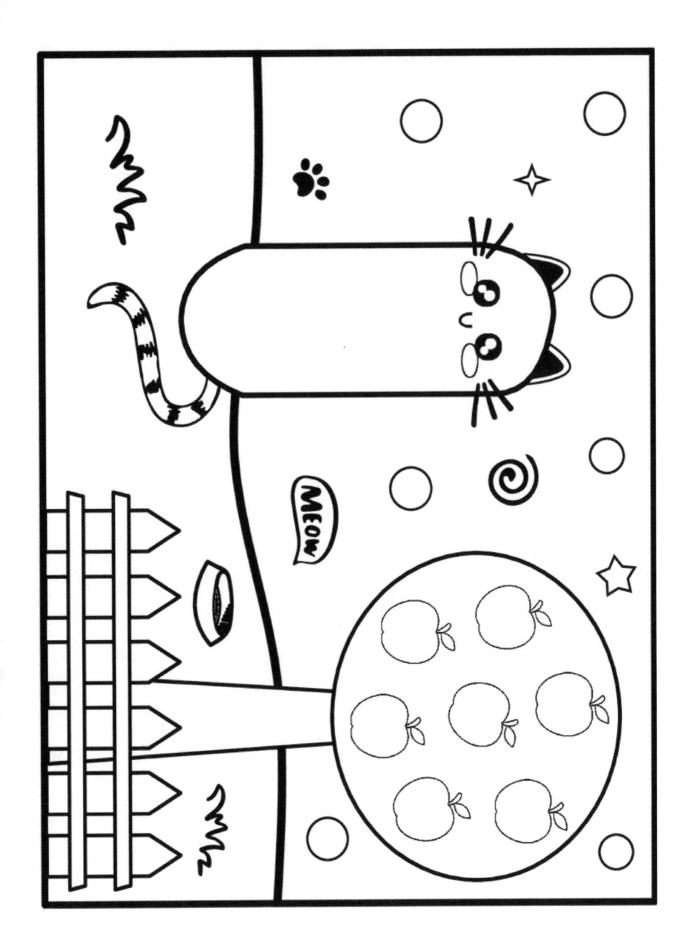

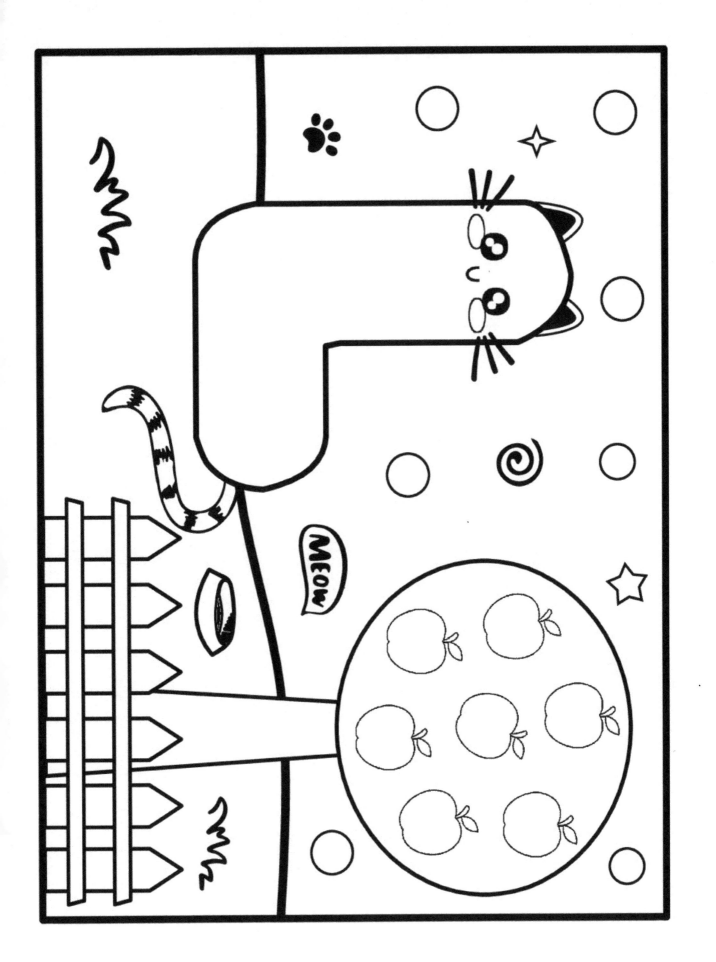

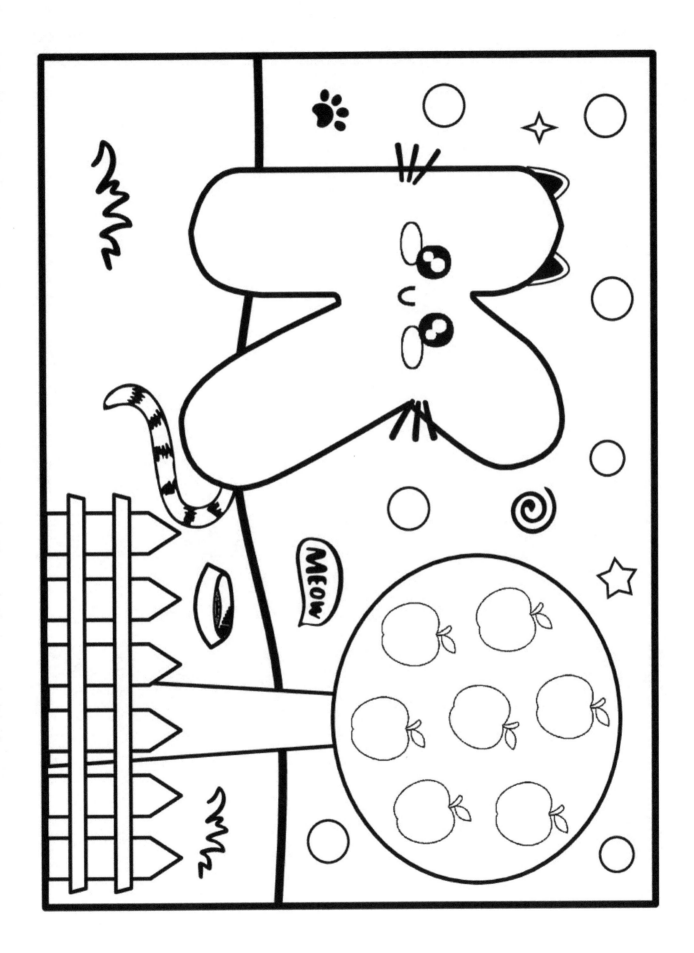

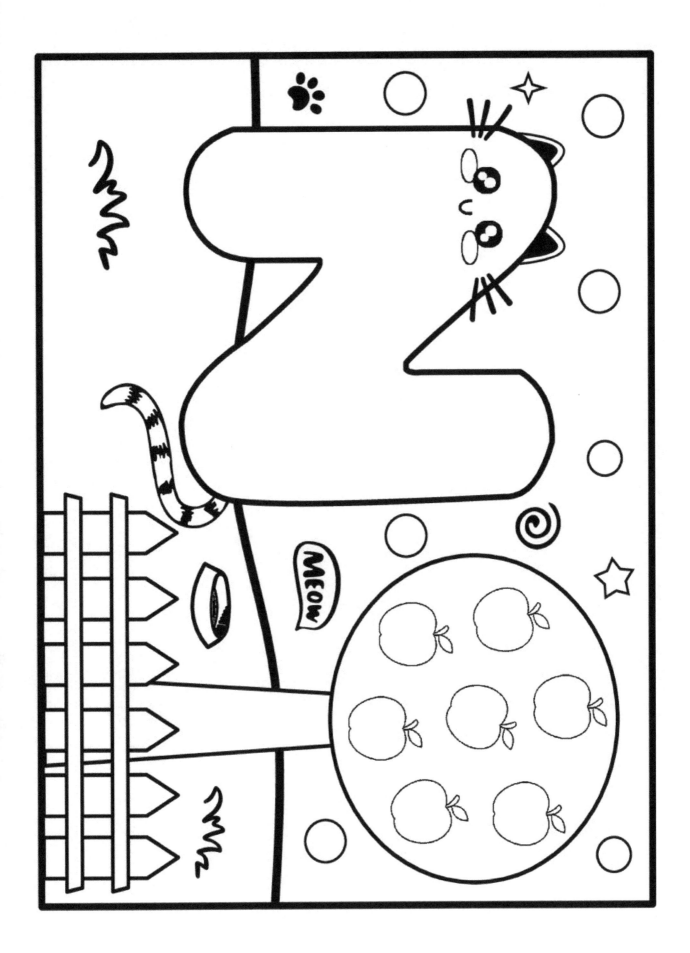

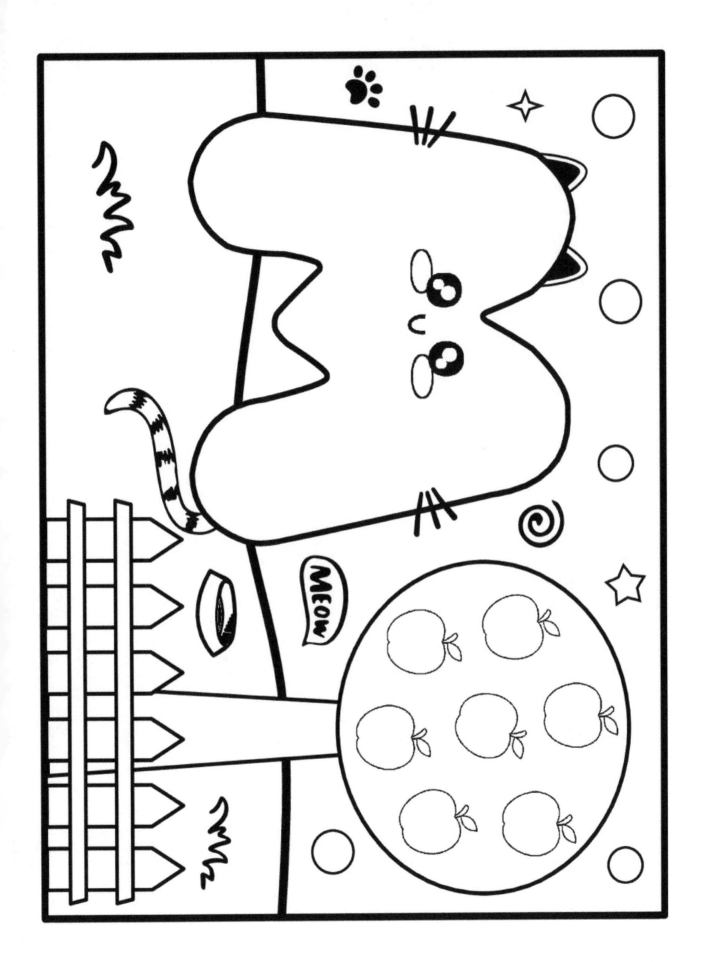

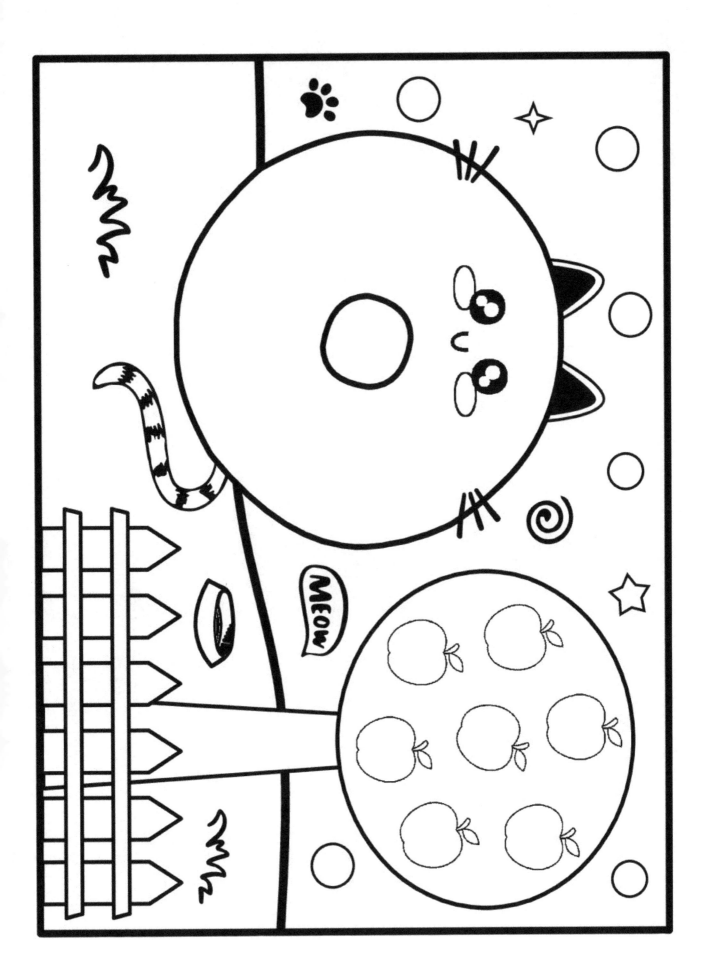

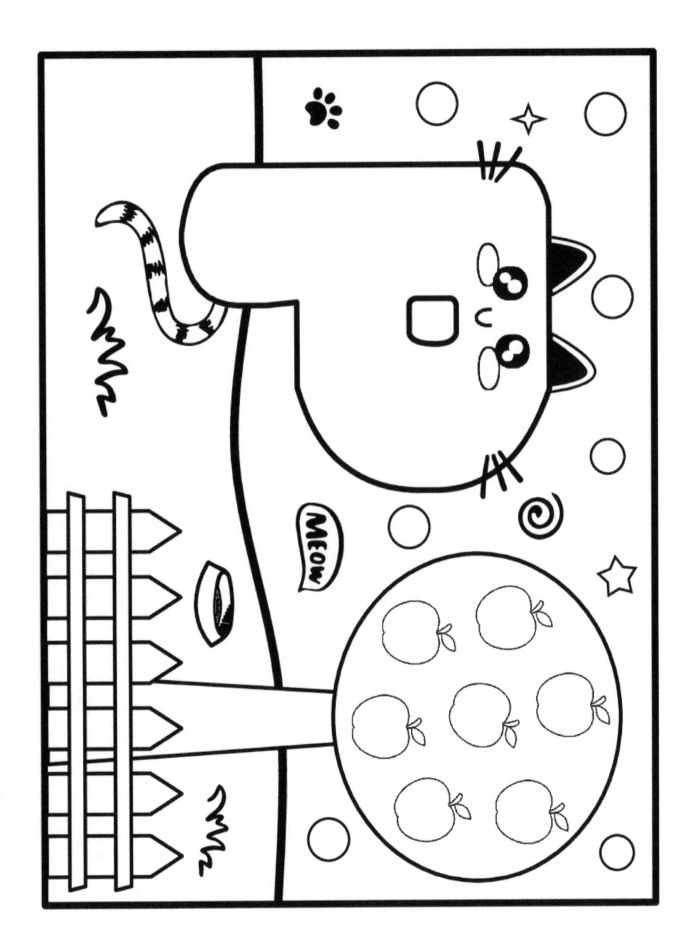

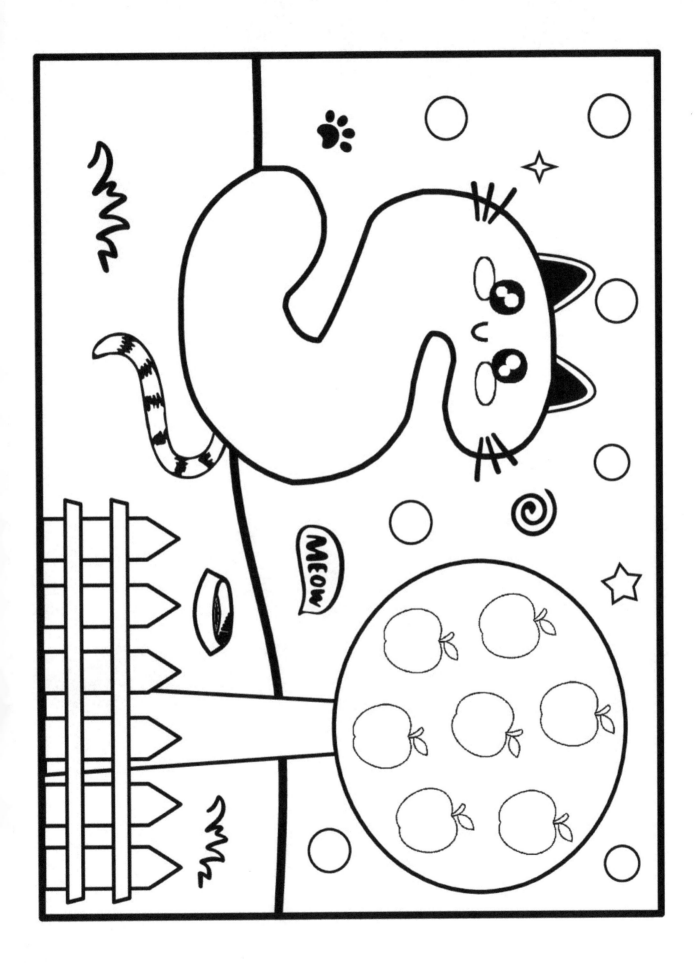

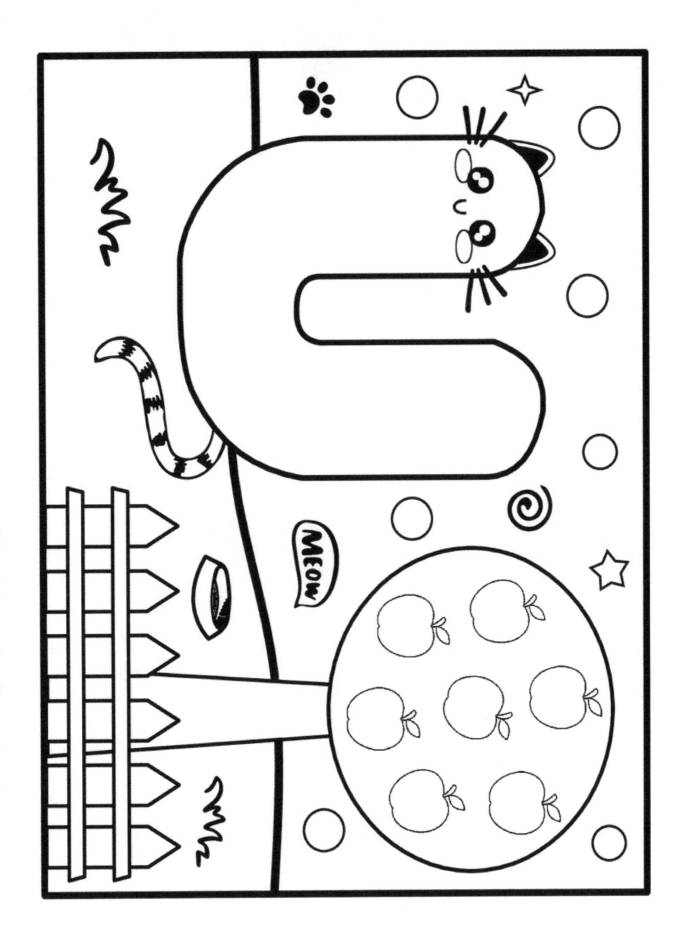

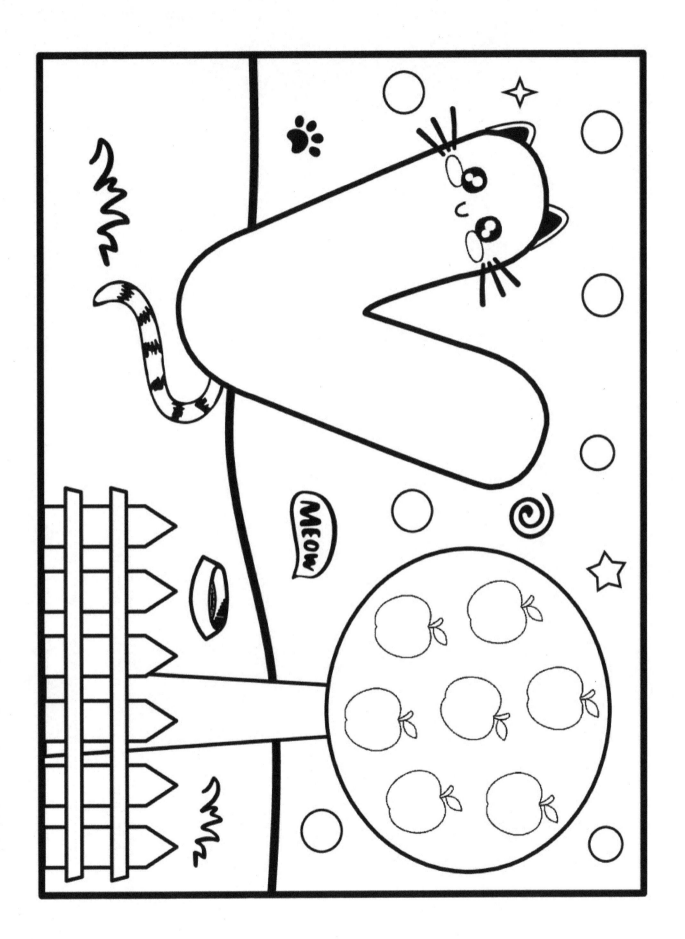

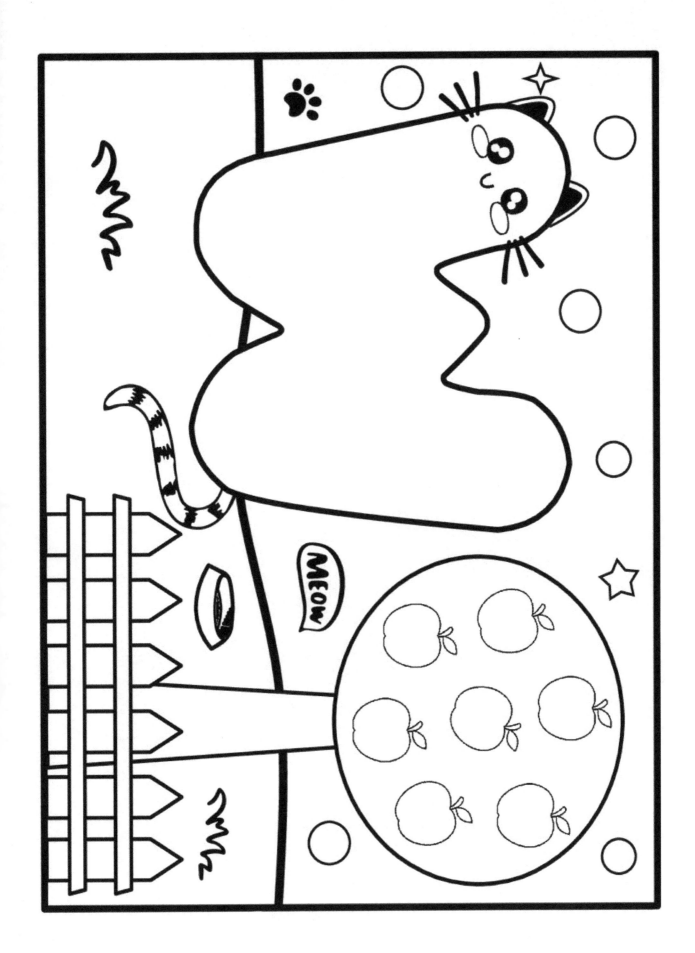

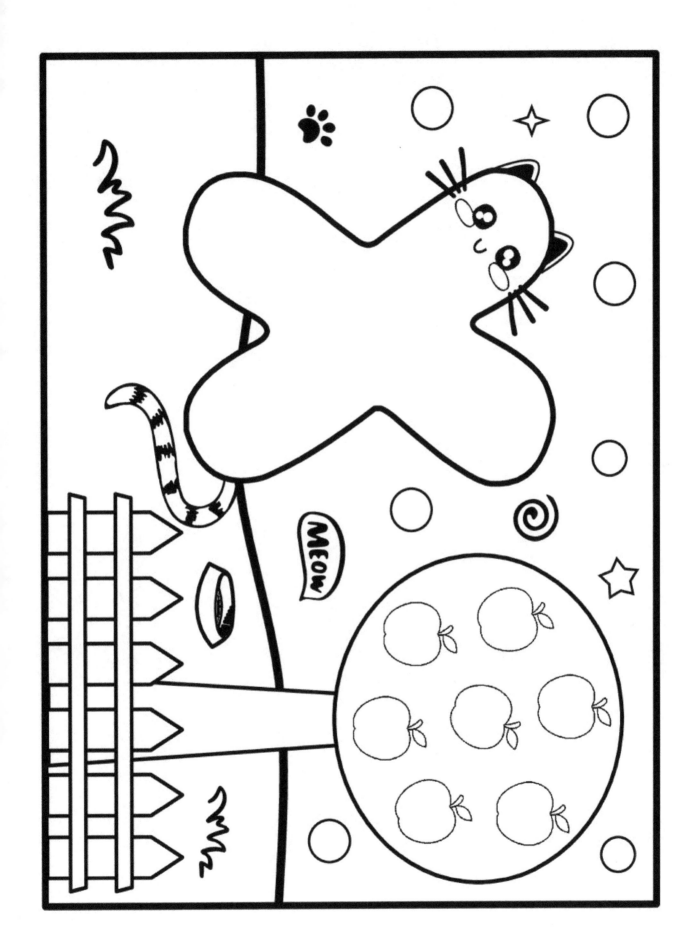

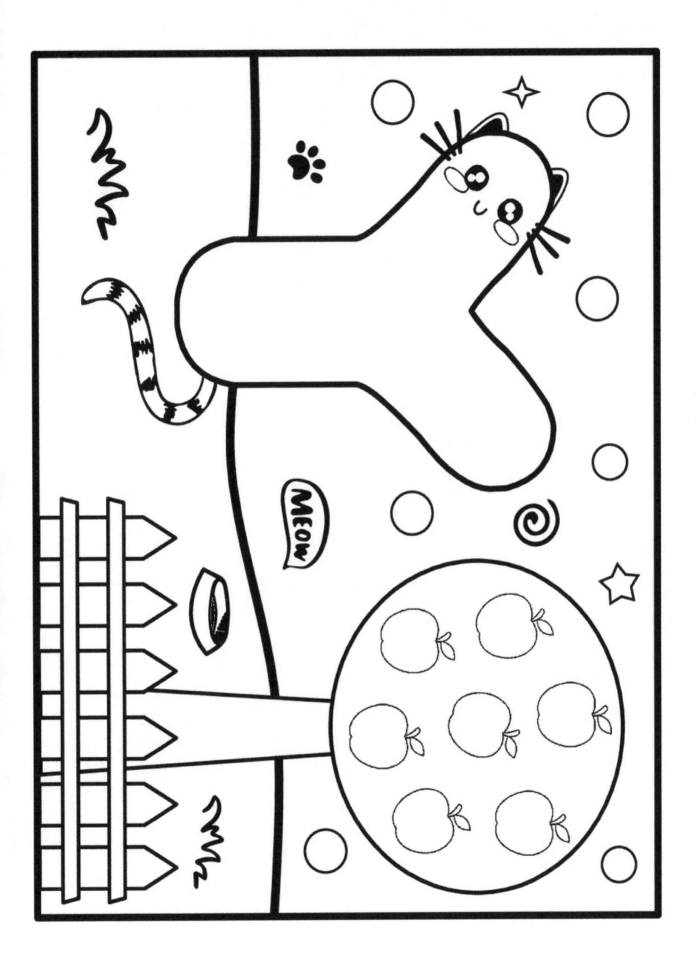

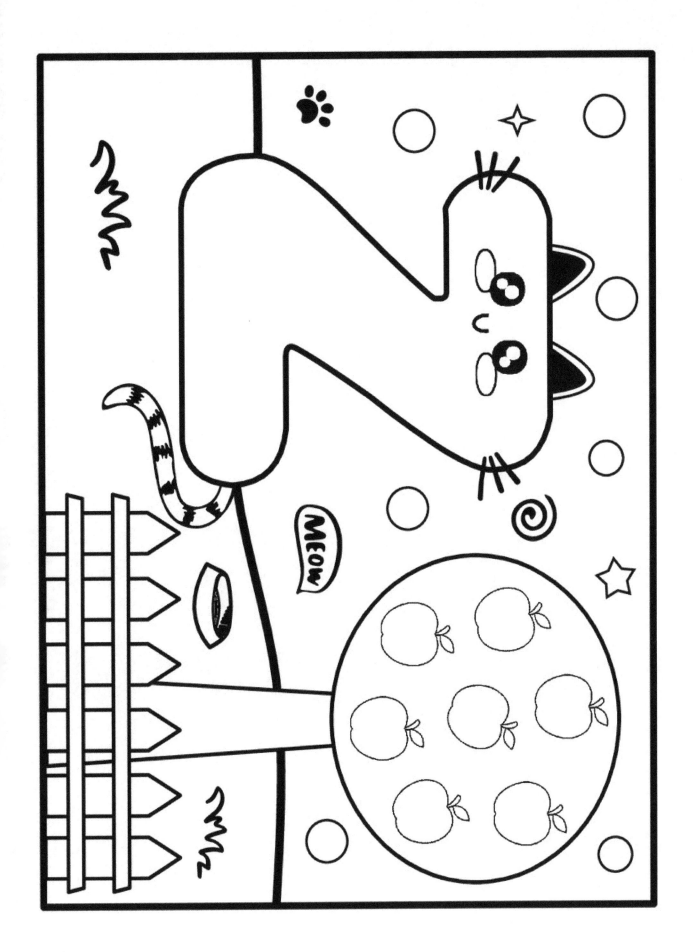

CPSIA information can be obtained
at www.ICGtesting.com
Printed in the USA
BVHW050228040521
606340BV00003B/794